Country Christmas

by
Eleanor Burns

to Grant and O
my favorite litt̶l̶e̶ ̶ ̶ ̶ ̶ ̶ ̶es
and to all my Family in Pennsylvania
who have always given a Country Christmas.

Contents

1. Door Bells

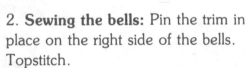

Materials:
½ yd. first calico
½ yd. second calico
⅓ yd. calico or eyelet yardage for bow
¼ yd. trim for first calico bell
½ yd. trim for second calico bells
1 yd. narrow ribbon (3 - 12" pieces)
3 jingle bells
1 lb. fiberfill
½ yd. bonded batting
1 plastic drapery ring

1. **Cutting:** *Bells* — Cut 2 bells from the first calico, and 4 bells from the second calico. Cut 3 bells from the bonded batting.
Bow — Cut 1 strip 10" x 14" and 1 strip 16" x 5" from the calico or eyelet. Cut a 7 x 10" piece and a 2½" x 16" piece from the bonded batting.

Ill. 1

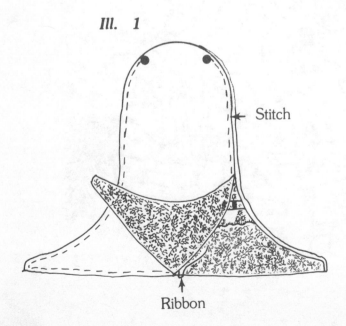

Stitch

Ribbon

2. **Sewing the bells:** Pin the trim in place on the right side of the bells. Topstitch.
3. Cut the ribbon into 3 - 12" pieces. Pin in place on the bottom of each bell.
4. Pin the 3 sets of bells right sides together with a batting bell pinned in place on the bottom. Stitch around the outside edge, leaving a 5" opening at the top. Turn. Poke out the points. *Ill. 1*
5. For a smooth front, stuff the bell behind the batting. Slip stitch the opening shut. Draw a bell up the ribbon and tie the ribbon into a bow.

6. Lay the 2 second calico bells beside each other with their tops and points touching. Whipstitch together at these points. *Ill. 2*

7. Lay the first calico bell on top. Drop it down 1½" from the top of the second calico bells. Whipstitch the top half of the bell to the two underneath. *Ill. 3*

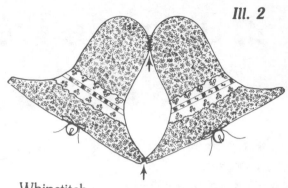

Ill. 2

Whipstitch

Ill. 3

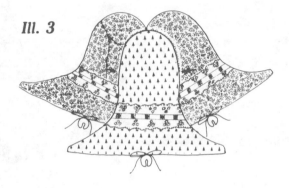

Ill. 4

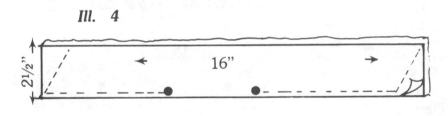

2½"   ← 16" →

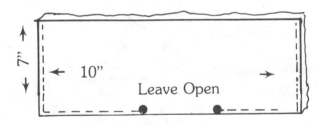

7"   ← 10" →
Leave Open

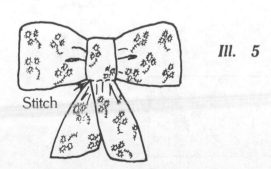

Stitch

Ill. 5

8. **Sewing the bow:** Fold the 10" x 14" piece and the 16" x 5 " in half. Pin the batting to the backs of the 2 folded pieces.

9. Stitch a ¼" seam, following the diagram. Turn the pieces through the holes. *Ill. 4*

10. Hand pleat the pieces through the centers and pin. Fold the long piece over the top of the rectangle. *Ill. 5*

11. Stitch through all thicknesses. Handstitch the bow to the top of the bells.

12. Handstitch a plastic drapery ring to the back for hanging.

2. Triangle Tree

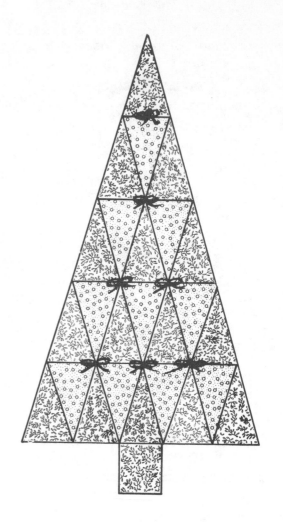

Materials:
¼ yd. main calico
¼ yd. second calico
⅔ yd. backing fabric
⅔ yd bonded batting
7 bells, balls or pompoms
OR 2⅔ yds. ribbon cut into 8 - 12"
   pieces
1 drapery ring

This tree is made of 25 trianges.
Fifteen — main calico
Ten — second calico

1. **Marking and Cutting:** Cut the calico
into 2 - 7" x 45" strips. Place the two
calicos right sides together with the main
color on the bottom.
2. Using the triangle pattern, mark and
cut 10 pairs of triangles, 5 main color
triangles, and 1 - 5" sq. from either
calico for the tree base. *Ill. 1*
3. Rearrange all 10 pairs of triangles. The
main color is on the bottom with the
point up. The second calico is right sides
together with the point down. *Ill. 2*

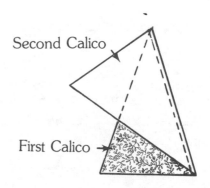

Second Calico

First Calico ➤

Ill. 2

Ill. 1

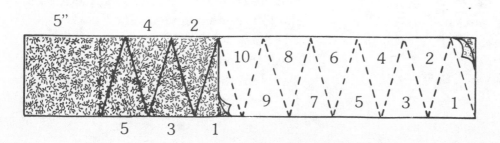

4. **Sewing:** Stitch and butt the 10 pairs of triangles together, using a ¼" seam allowance. Snip the threads between the pairs. Unfold the pairs. *Ill. 3*

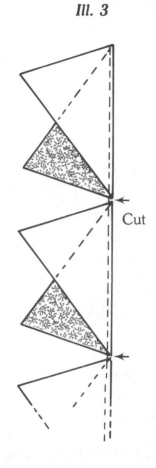

Cut

Ill. 4

5. Stitch and butt the pairs and main calico singles together until 4 rows are sewn. **Ill. 4**

6. **Tree:** Sew the top triangle and the 4 rows together to form the tree.

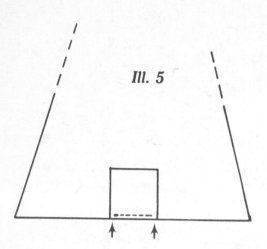

Ill. 5

7. **Base of tree:** Sew the 5" square to the center of the bottom of the tree, leaving ¼" free on each side. *Ill. 5*

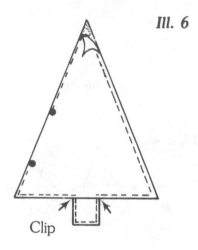

Ill. 6

Clip

8. **Lining:** Pin the triangle tree and lining right sides together. Cut the lining the same size as the tree. Cut the bonded batting ¼" less on all sides.

9. Stitch around the outside edge, leaving a 4" opening on one side for turning. Clip at the corners of the base. *Ill. 6*

10. Turn. Slip the batting in between the backing and the tree. Whipstitch the opening shut.

11. **Decorations:** Handstitch on the bells, balls or pompoms through all thicknesses. Stitch a drapery ring on the back for hanging.

OR

12. **Ribbon Bows:** Starting at the top and working down, lay the ribbon flat in place. Stitch back and forth across the ribbon through all thicknesses. Lift the pressure foot and move to the next ribbon. Cut the threads on the back all at one time. Tie the ribbon into bows. *Ill. 7*

13. **Ribbon Hanger:** Lay a piece of ribbon across the back in exactly the same place as the ribbon in the top front. Stitch both at the same time.

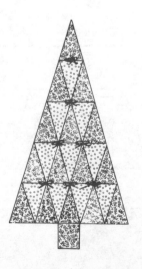

Ill. 7

3. Tree Top Star

Materials:
1 - 2¾" x 20" strip first calico
1 - 2¾" x 20" strip second calico
12" sq. backing fabric
¼ lb. fiberfill stuffing
¾ yd. of 5/8" ribbon
1 plastic drapery ring

1. **Sewing:** Place 2 strips right sides together. Seam one side with a ¼" seam allowance.
2. Mark and cut the star pattern 4 times.
Ill. 1

Ill. 1

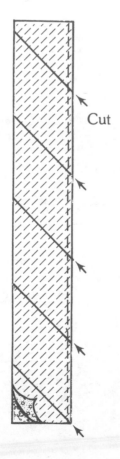

Cut

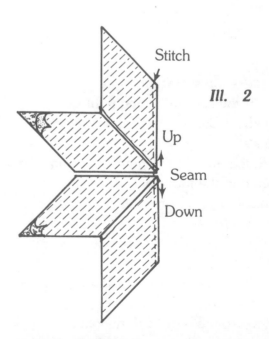

Stitch

Ill. 2

Up

Seam

Down

3. Unfold 2 pairs, place right sides together and stitch 1 side. Fold the seam up. *Ill. 2*
4. Butt and sew on the second set of pairs. Fold the seam down.

5. Refold and stitch across the middle.
Ill. 3

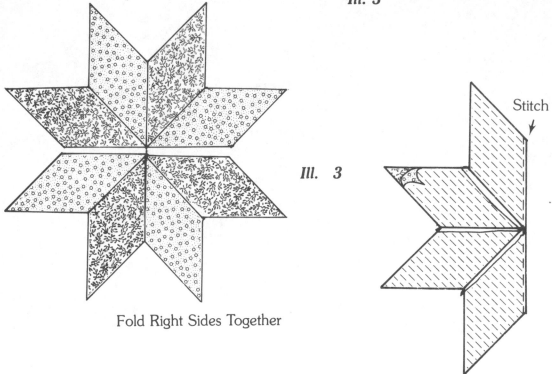

Ill. 3

Fold Right Sides Together

Stitch

6. Press the seams flat.
7. Pin the star and lining right sides together. Cut the lining the same size as the star.
8. Stitch around the points, leaving the needle in the fabric and pivoting at each point. Leave an opening on one side for turning. *Ill. 4*
9. Clip. Turn. Stuff. Whipstitch the opening shut.
10. Lay the ribbon across the middle of the star.
11. From the back with needle and thread, draw through the middle of the star, stitch across the ribbon and knot from behind.
12. Tie the ribbon into a bow.
13. Handtack on a drapery ring for hanging.

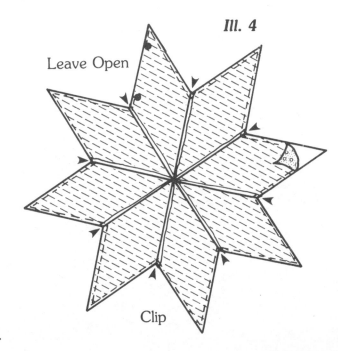

Ill. 4

Leave Open

Clip

10

4. Flying Angel

Materials:

Angel Body — ¼ yd. red calico

Wings and Apron — ¼ yd. lace or
  eyelet yardage (may need to be lined)

2 yds. pre-gathered narrow lace trim

4 - 12" pieces of ribbon

Hands, Legs, and Face — ¼ yd. pink or
  white solid color fabric

Facial Features — 2 - ½" shank button
  eyes, red embroidery floss for mouth

2 - 1½" flower appliques for cheeks

½" heart applique for nose

Hair — 1 skein rug yarn

l lb. polyester fiberfill stuffing

White plastic drapery ring

1. **Cutting:** Cut out pieces according to materials list and pattern instructions.
2. **Sewing:** Apron — Trim 2 edges with lace. Pin the apron in place across the top part of the body.
3. **Hands:** Sew the hands to the arms on both pieces. Flashfeed.

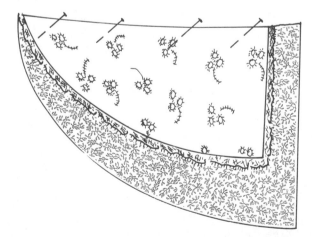

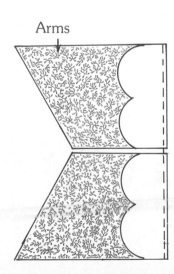

Arms

Right Sides
Together

4. Arms and Legs: Topstitch trim on the front sides of both pieces. Flashfeed. *Ill. 3*

Cut apart. Sew the pairs with right sides together. Leave the ends open. Clip at the points. Turn. Stuff lightly. Lay a 12" piece of ribbon across each quilting line. Machine stitch through all thicknesses on the quilting line. Pin and machine baste in place on the body. *Ill. 4*

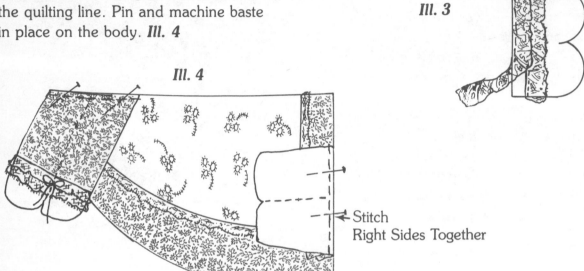

Ill. 3

Ill. 4

Stitch Right Sides Together

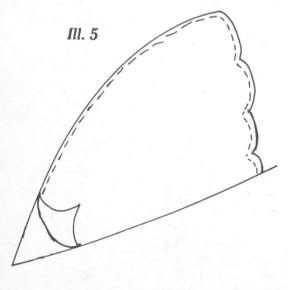

Ill. 5

5. Wings: With right sides together, stitch around the curved edges. Clip in at the points. Turn. *Ill. 5* Stuff lightly. Machine quilt through all thicknesses. Pin and machine baste in place on the top of the body. *Ill. 6*

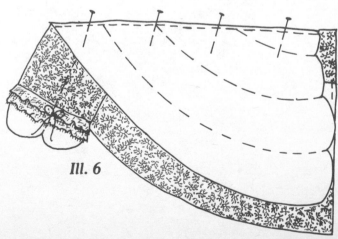

Ill. 6

6. **Body:** Place the second body piece on top with right sides together. Stitch around the body, leaving an opening under the arms. Turn. Stuff. Whipstitch the opening shut. *Ill. 7*

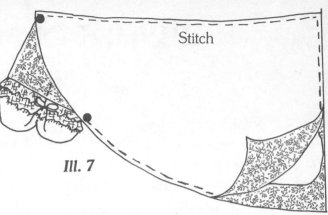

Stitch

Ill. 7

7. **Mouth:** Draw the mouth line on the face with a pencil. Change the top thread to red. Machine chain-stitch the outline of the mouth with an 18" piece of red embroidery floss. Put the sewing machine needle in the face fabric on one end of the mouth. Loop the floss behind the needle, back stitch to anchor, and hold equal ends of the floss taunt. Take 3 machine stitches. Criss-cross the floss in front of the needle. Take 3 machine stitches. Criss-cross the floss. Continue to stitch and criss-cross the floss until the mouth is stitched. Backstitch over the last chain to anchor. *Ill. 8*

9. **Hair**: Wrap the rug yarn around a 30" piece of cardboard. Knot the ends. Machine stitch the center part of the hair through all thicknesses. Hand stitch or glue the hair to the face. Machine tack 2 ribbons to the sides of the face. Tie the hair into "pigtails." Slip your fingers into the ends of the hair and twist toward the face. Tie into big knots. Tack the ends of the knots to the cheeks. *Ill. 9*

Handtack the head to the body. Hand tack a drapery ring to the back for hanging.

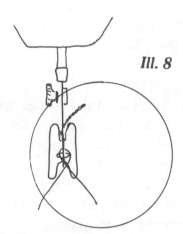

Ill. 8

Criss-Cross Embroidery Floss

8. **Face:** Sew on the cheek appliques to cover the raw ends of the embroidery floss mouth. Sew on the heart applique nose and button eyes. With right sides together, stitch around the outside edge of the head. Leave an opening at the top. Turn. Stuff. Whipstitch the opening shut.

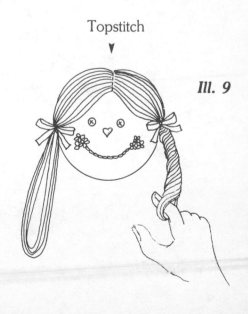

Topstitch

Ill. 9

5. Patchwork Stockings

Calico Strip Stocking
Materials for Front
Approximately 10 - 12" strips of calico
  (1", 2", and 3" wide)
Crazy Quilt Stocking
Materials for Front
Assorted scraps of red and green calico
  (any shape, approximately 2" x 3")
Materials for Both Stockings:
½ yd. backing fabric
¼ yd. contrast fabric for cuff
½ yd. lining fabric (muslin or sheeting)
15" x 20" piece of bonded batting
⅔ yd. ribbon

1. **Cutting for both stockings:** Cut 1
stocking from the backing fabric, 2 from
the lining and 1 from the bonded batting.
Cut 1 cuff 7" x 14".

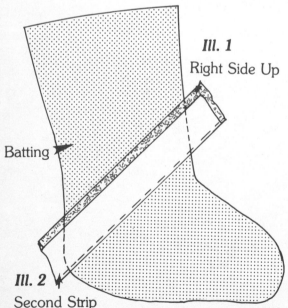

Ill. 1
Right Side Up

Batting

Ill. 2
Second Strip

2. **Sewing the front of the Calico Strip
Stocking:** Lay the first strip right side up
at an angle on the bonded batting. Do
not trim the strip. *Ill. 1*
3. Lay the second strip to it right sides
together. Allow extra strip to hang over
on both sides. Stitch through all
thicknesses. Unfold and fingerpress. *Ill. 2*
4. Lay on the third strip right sides
together, stitch through all thicknesses,
unfold and fingerpress.

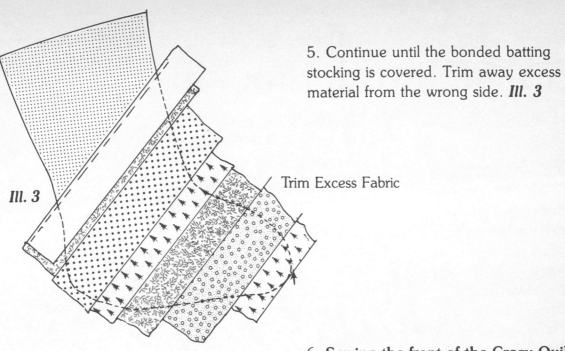

5. Continue until the bonded batting stocking is covered. Trim away excess material from the wrong side. *Ill. 3*

Ill. 3

Trim Excess Fabric

6. **Sewing the front of the Crazy Quilt Stocking:** Sort small scraps into a pile of red and a pile of green.

7. Pick up one red piece and one green piece. Match and stitch straight equal sides of the two pieces with right sides together. Flag pairs by stitching from one pair to the next without lifting the pressure foot or cutting the pairs apart. *Ill. 4*

8. After stitching many pairs, cut apart and stitch the pairs together, until the pairs are wide enough for rows to fit across the bonded batting. *Ill. 5*

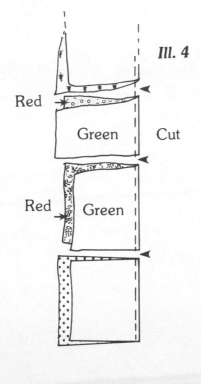

Ill. 4

Red

Green   Cut

Red

Green

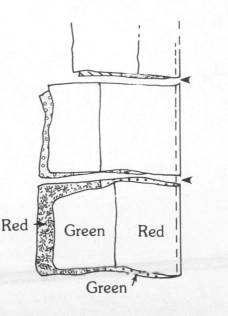

Ill. 5

Red   Green   Red

Green

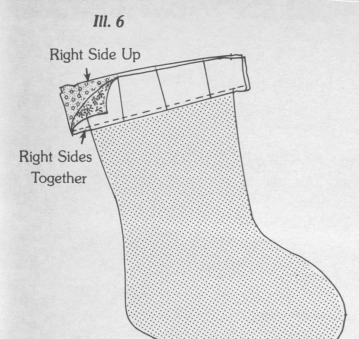

Ill. 6

Right Side Up

Right Sides
Together

9. Place the first row right side up on top of the batting at the top of the stocking. Place the second row on top right sides together and stitch through all thicknesses. Unfold and fingerpress. **Ill. 6**

10. Add the next rows until all the batting is completely covered. Trim all the ends away from the wrong side.

11. **Sewing assembly for both Stockings:** Place the back of the stocking and the patchwork stocking right sides together. Place the two linings right sides together. Stack on top of each other, with the batting on the bottom. **Ill. 7**

12. Stitch around the outside edge with a ¼" seam allowance. Turn right side out.

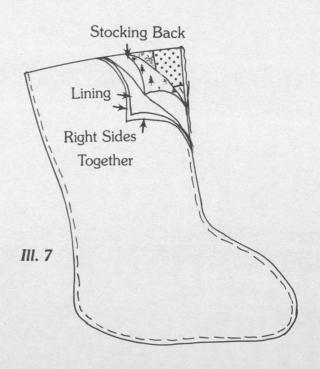

Stocking Back

Lining

Right Sides
Together

Ill. 7

Ill. 8

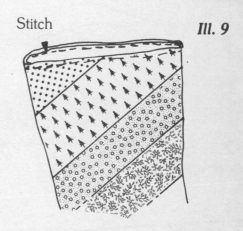

Fold

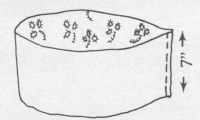

13. Cuff: Fold the 7" x 14" piece in half, right sides together. Stitch the 7" side. Turn right side out and fold in half the other way to form a circle. The seam is now on the inside. *Ill. 8*

14. Drop the cuff into the center of the stocking, match the raw edges, right sides together, and stitch around the top of the cuff. *Ill. 9*

15. Fold the cuff back up and over the top of the stocking.

Stitch   *Ill. 9*

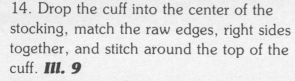

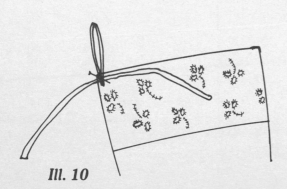

Ill. 10

16. Hanger: Loop and pin an 8" piece of ribbon in the upper left hand corner of the stocking. Lay a 16" piece of ribbon across it and stitch through all thicknesses. *Ill. 10*

17. Tie the ribbon into a bow.

6. Calico Tree Skirt

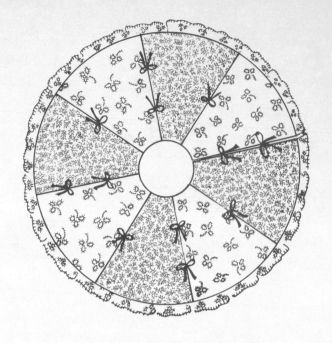

Materials:

1¼ yds. first calico

1¼ yds. second calico or solid color

1⅔ yds. lining

1⅔ yds. bonded batting

4½ yds. eyelet lace

4⅔ yds. ribbon in red or green cut into
   14 - 12" pieces

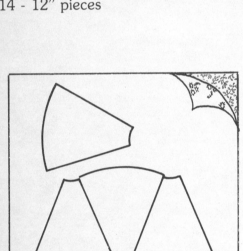
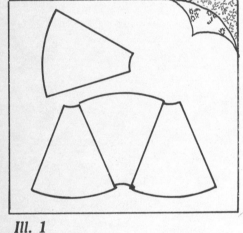

Ill. 1

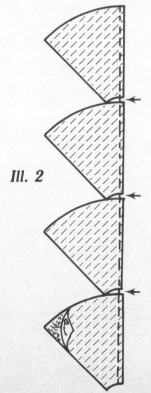

Ill. 2

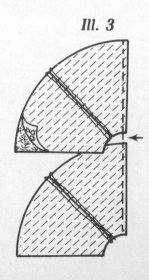

Ill. 3

1. **Cutting:** Lay the first calico and second calico right sides together. Cut 4 gores from each. *Ill. 1*

2. **Sewing:** With right sides together, flash feed 4 sets of gores using ¼" seam allowance. Always have the same color on the top. *Ill. 2*

3. Seam the 2 pairs into halves. *Ill. 3*

4. Using the pieced section as a pattern, cut 2 half sections from batting and 2 half sections from the lining. **Ill. 4**

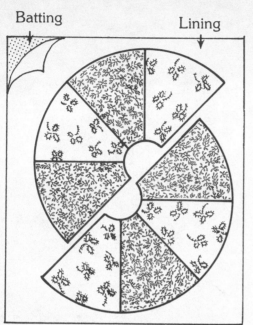

Batting   Lining

Ill. 4

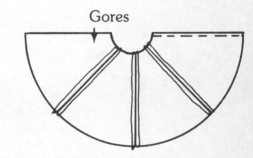

Gores

Ill. 5

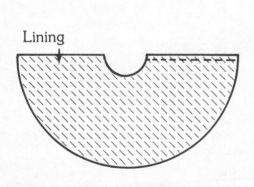

Lining

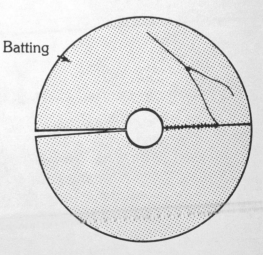

Batting

5. Stitch 1 seam on the gores and lining separately. Press the seams open. Butt and whip stitch the batting together. **Ill. 5**

6. Lay the 3 circles flat on the floor and pin together. Place the batting down first, lining right side up, eyelet lace around the outside curved edge, and the pieced gore circle on top with right side down.
7. Stitch through all three layers. Leave an opening for turning. *Ill. 6*
8. Turn. Pin the raw edges in.

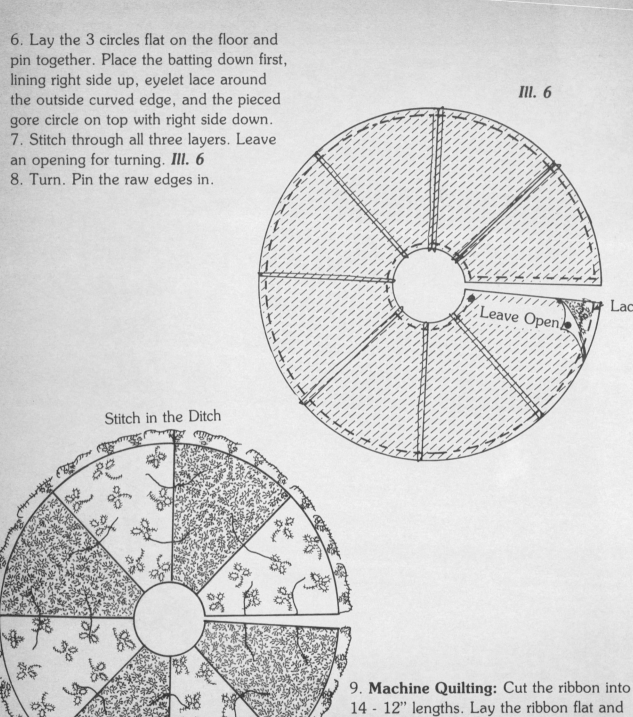

Ill. 6

Leave Open

Lace

Stitch in the Ditch

Ill. 7

9. **Machine Quilting:** Cut the ribbon into 14 - 12" lengths. Lay the ribbon flat and perpendicular to the seam. Pin in place. "Stitch in the ditch" through all layers and ribbons, starting at the outer edge and stitching to the middle. *Ill. 7*

10. Machine edge-stitch the straight sides and tack on the bows.

11. Tie the ribbons into bows.

7. Padded Door Wreath

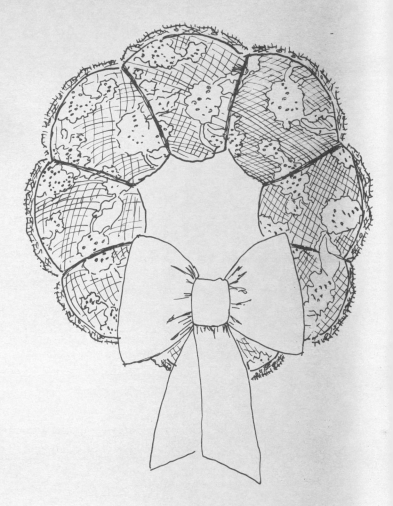

Materials:

½ yd. over-all lace yardage
¾ yd. solid color fabric
1¼ yd. pre-gathered 1½" wide lace trim
¾ yd. bonded batting
3½ yd. narrow ribbon
12" styrofoam circle or cardboard circle with 8" center cut out for wreath base.

1. **Cutting the wreath:** Cut the over-all lace into 1 — 15" x 45" piece. Cut the solid color fabric into 1 — 15" x 45" piece for the wreath and 10" x 14" and 16" x 5" pieces for the padded bow. Cut the ribbon into 8 — 15" pieces and 1 — 6" piece. Cut the batting into 2 — 12" x 48" pieces for padding the wreath and 7" x 10" and 2½" x 16" pieces for padding the bow.

2. *Sewing the wreath:* Lay the overall lace fabric on top of the solid color fabric with both right sides up. Pin together.
3. Sew the lace trim on 1 long side, right sides together. Baste the opposite long edge to hold the 2 layers together. *Ill. 1*

Ill. 1

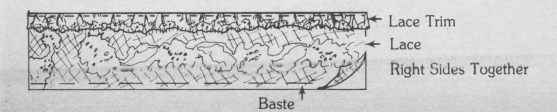

← Lace Trim

← Lace

Right Sides Together

Baste ↑

4. Refold with short sides right sides together. Fold and pin the seam allowance in toward the fabric. Fold the lace out. Sew the short ends together. *Ill. 2*

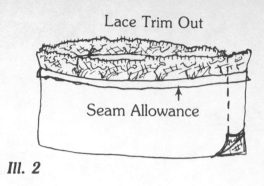

Lace Trim Out

Seam Allowance

Ill. 2

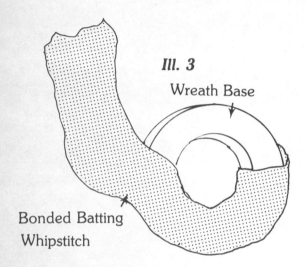

Ill. 3

Wreath Base

Bonded Batting
Whipstitch

5. Wrap the bonded batting around the wreath base. Whipstitch loosely. *Ill. 3*
6. Push the fabric circle into the center of the padded circle. Wrap around so that the lace trim lays around the outside edge.

Pin in Edges
Overlap Lace 1/8"

Ill. 4

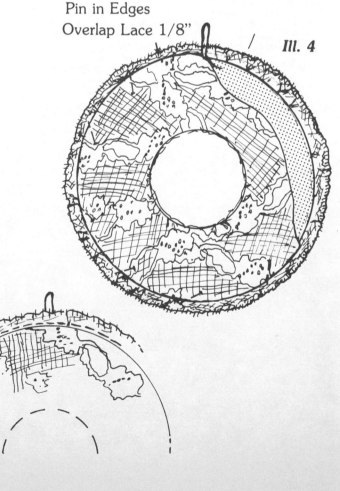

7. Turn the raw edge under and pin the edges together. Overlap on the back 1/8". Insert a 6" loop for hanging between the two layers. Machine stitch in the ditch from the front. *Ill. 4*
8. Evenly space and tie from behind the 8 — 15" pieces of ribbon.
9. Follow the instructions for making the bow in the Door Bell pattern.
10. Hand tack the bow in place

Stitch in the Ditch

8. Red-Nosed Reindeer

Materials:

Body and Ears — ⅓ yd. brown calico
(enough for 2)

Underbody — ¼ yd. light red calico

Antlers — 1/8 yd. yellow calico

Eyes — 2 buttons

Nose — 1 red button or red pompom

Tail — 1 white pompom

1 jingle bell

½ yd. ribbon

½ lb. fiberfill stuffing

1. **Cutting:** Cut 2 brown bodies, 2 light red underbodies, 4 yellow antlers, 2 brown ears and 2 light red ears.

2. **Sewing the eyes:** Sew on the button eyes by hand or machine.

Speed Sew method of sewing buttons on with a zigzag sewing machine: Sew the stitch length at 0. Set the zigzag width on medium or as wide apart as the holes are. Tape the buttons in place. Drop the pressure foot on top of the button. Let the machine zigzag back and forth into the holes several times. Clip the threads.

3. **Sewing the body:** Place the two bodies right sides together. Stitch from the point under the neck to the point under the tail.

4. **Sewing the underbody:** Fold over and sew in the darts on the wrong side. Flashfeed and sew all four in a series. Clip the threads in between each. *Ill. 1*

Stitch

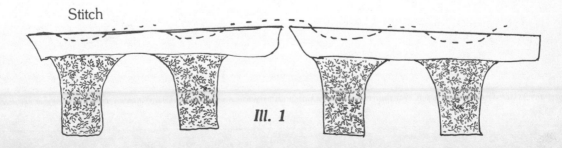

Ill. 1

Place the two pieces right sides together. Stitch the long top side, leave a 4" opening for turning and stuffing. **Ill. 2**

5. Pin together the deer body (on the bottom) and the underbody (on the top) with right sides together. Match the front point under the neck and back point under the tail.

Leave Open

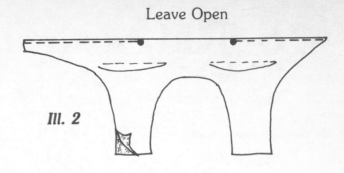

Ill. 2

Ill. 3

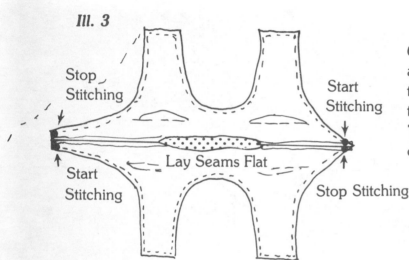

Stop Stitching

Start Stitching

Lay Seams Flat

Start Stitching

Stop Stitching

6. Start stitching at the neck to the tail, and cut the threads. Begin stitching on the other side of the tail, and stitch back to the point at the neck. **Ill. 3**

7. Turn. Stuff firmly. Whipstitch the opening shut.

8. **Sewing the ears and antlers:** (2 pairs of each). Place the right sides together. Stitch, leaving open at the bottom. Turn. Stuff the antlers firmly.
Pin a tuck in the ears.

9. Pin the ears in place on the body. Turn under the raw edges on the antlers and pin in place over the ends of the ears. Whipstitch the antlers and ears to the body. **Ill. 4**

10. Hand sew on the nose and tail.

11. Wrap the ribbon around the deer's neck. Slip on the bell. Tie the ribbon into a bow.

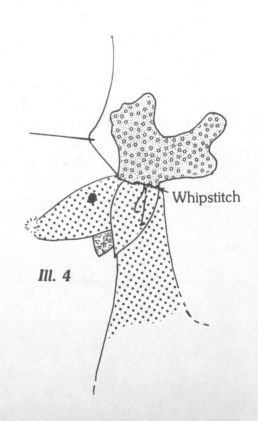

Whipstitch

Ill. 4

9. Jolly Santa

Materials:
½ yd. red fabric
⅛ yd. short white fur fabric
1/8 yd. brown calico for bag
1 yd. string
1 lb. fiberfill stuffing
1 sq. felt for mittens and boots
¼ yd. long curly white fur fabric
1 nylon stocking
2 shank button eyes
1 jingle bell
Scraps of pink and red felt
1 jingle bell

1. **Cutting Santa:** Cut 1 jacket, 1 hat and 1 pants on the fold. Cut   mittens and 2 boots. Cut fur strips 1" x 9" and 2" x 55". Cut the brown calico bag in 2 — 4½" x 10" pieces.

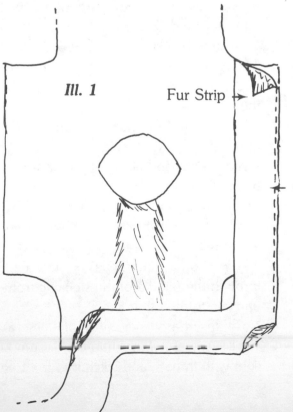

Ill. 1

Fur Strip →

Right Sides Together

← Cuff

2. **Sewing the Jacket:** Topstitch the 1" fur strip down the front of the jacket.
3. Sew the 2" x 55" strip of fur on the cuffs, bottom of the jacket, and bottom of the hat. Flashfeed by sewing continuously and bending the cuffs, hat and bottom of the jacket onto the strip. Cut the strip apart. *Ill. 1*

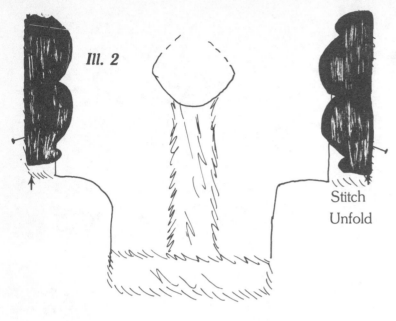

Ill. 2

Stitch
Unfold

4. Sew the mittens on the ends of the cuffs. *Ill. 2*

5. Fold the jacket right sides together. Sew from the top fold of the mitten to the hemline. Turn right side out.

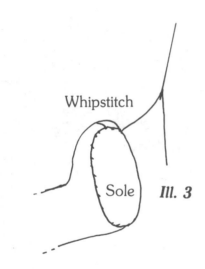

Whipstitch

Sole   *Ill. 3*

6. **Sewing the Boots:** Sew the front seam of the boot. Turn. Stuff. Whipstitch the sole in place. *Ill. 3*

7. **Sewing the Pants:** Sew the center back seam. Pin the boots in place on the bottom of each cuff. *Ill. 4*

8. Sew across the bottom of the cuffs and crotch. Turn.

9. Place the jacket front and pants front right sides together. Sew.

10. Stuff the arms, legs, and body.

11. Pull the back of Santa's jacket down over his backside and whipstitch. Whipstitch the underarms to the body.

12. **Sewing the Head:** Stuff the toe section of the stocking to the size of a baseball. Wrap, gather and tie off at the base of the head. Trim off to 3″.
Stuff the bottom of the stocking into the body of Santa. Whipstitch the head securely to the body.

13. Sew on 2 button eyes by stitching through the middle of the stocking from one eye to the other.
Nose: Insert a ¾″ wad of stuffing into a small piece of nylon, wrap the bottom off tight with thread, and stitch it to the face.

Ill. 4

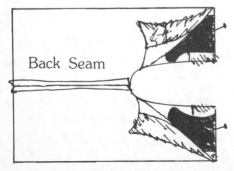

Back Seam

14. **Cutting the Whiskers:** Make a paper pattern triangle and fit to Santa. Cut the triangle from the curly fur.

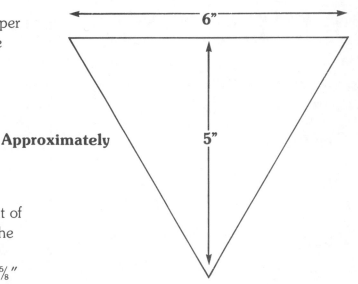

Approximately 6" 5"

15. Handstitch the whiskers to the front of the face, and a second strip section in the back for hair.

16. Glue on a red felt mouth and two ⅝" pink felt circles for cheeks.

17. **Sewing the Hat:** Fold right sides together. Sew one side. Turn. Whipstitch the hat to the head. Pull the top of the hat down at an angle and sew on the jingle bell.

Wrong Sides Together   *Ill. 6*

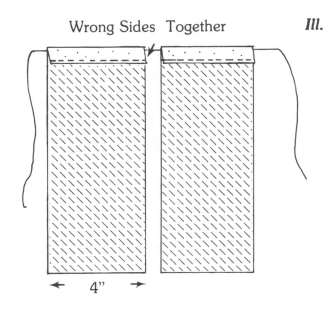

4"

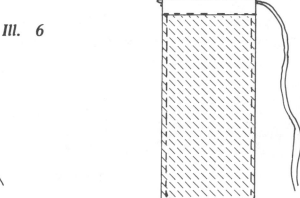

18. **Sewing the Bag:** Fold ¼" over the string on the 4" side with wrong sides together. Edgestitch. *Ill. 6*

19. Place right sides together. Stitch the sides and bottom. Curve the bottom with stitching. Trim the curves. Turn.

20. Stuff with fiberfill on the bottom of the bag and tiny wrapped presents on the top of the bag.

21. Wrap the string around Santa's arm and let the bag hang down his back.

10. Tree Ornaments

Christmas Mouse

He loves to peek out of the top of stockings!

Materials:
1/8 yd. white fur fabric
1 sq. pink felt
2 black beads for eyes
10" carpet thread
Handful fiberfill stuffing

1. **Cutting the mouse:** Cut 2 bodies from the fur. Cut 2 ears, a tail and base from the pink felt.
2. **Sewing the mouse:** Sew on the bead eyes. Tuck and machine stitch the ears to the body. Pin the tail in place. ***Ill. 1***

Ill. 1

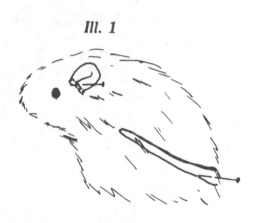

Ill. 2

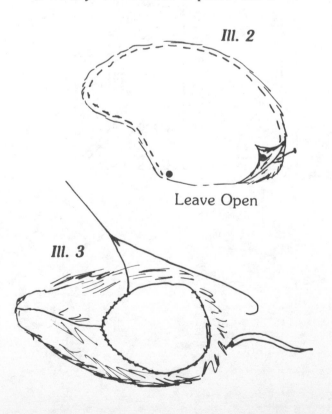

Leave Open

3. Place the 2 bodies right sides together. Leave open on the bottom. Stitch. Turn. ***Ill. 2***
4. Stuff firmly from the bottom.
5. Whipstitch the base to the bottom of the mouse.
6. Draw a double strand of carpet thread through for whiskers. Clip to size. ***Ill. 3***

Ill. 3

Holly Berry Ornament

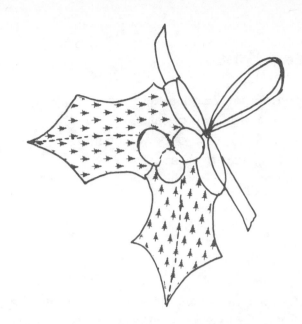

Decorate the tops of stockings, packages and the tree with holly berries.

Materials:
Scrap of green fabric
Scrap of red fabric
7" x 7" piece of bonded batting
¾ yd. ribbon

1. **Cutting the Holly:** Cut 2 pairs of holly leaves from the green. Cut 2 from the bonded batting. Cut 3 circles from the red for berries.

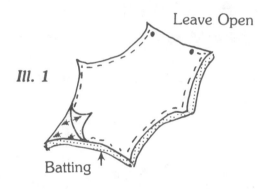

Ill. 1

Leave Open

Batting ↑

2. **Sewing the leaves:** Place a pair of leaves right sides together, with a batting leaf on the bottom. *Ill. 1*
3. Stitch around the outside edge, leaving an opening for turning near the stem. Turn.
4. Whipstitch the opening shut. Machine topstitch with green thread.

5. **Sewing the berries:** Run a gathering stitch around the outside edge. Stuff and draw up tightly. Handstitch the 3 berries to the top of the 2 leaves. **Ill. 2**
6. **Sewing the ribbon loop:** Make a loop with 6" of ribbon. Lay 21" of ribbon across the bottom of the loop. Stitch. **Ill. 3**
7. Sew the loop to the leaves and berries. Tie the ribbon into a bow.

Ill. 2

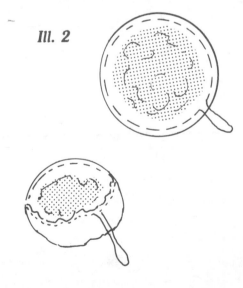

Ribbon

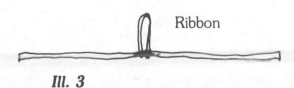

Ill. 3

Tree Bows

Materials for Two Bows:
1 — 6" x 45" strip of calico
1 — 6" x 45" strip of bonded batting
2 — 6" pieces of wire
(Refer to bow illustrations with the Door Bells pattern.)

1. **Cutting the bows:** Divide the strip into 4 equal pieces 11" each.
2. Fold 2 crosswise and 2 lengthwise. Cut the batting the same size as the 2 folded pieces. Pin the batting to the backs of each.
3. **Sewing the bows:** Stitch, following the illustrations with the Door Bells pattern.
4. Turn and pleat both pieces through the centers.
5. Fold the long piece over the top of the rectangle. Stitch through all thicknesses.
6. Run piece of wire through the back of the bow to attach the bow to the tree branches.
7. This bow is perfect for trimming packages.

Tree Star

Materials:
1 — 2¼" x 14" strip first calico
1 — 2¼" x 14" strip second calico
10" sq. backing fabric
Handful fiberfill stuffing
½ yd. narrow ribbon
8" strand yarn

1. Follow cutting and sewing instructions for the Tree Top Star.
2. Run a strand of yarn through the back and tie for hanging.

Order Information:

If you do not have a fine quilt shop in your area, you may write for a complete catalog and current price list of all books and patterns published by Quilt in a Day.

Books

Quilt in a Day Log Cabin
The Sampler -- A Machine Sewn Quilt
Trio of Treasured Quilts
Lover's Knot Quilt
Amish Quilt in a Day
Irish Chain in a Day
May Basket Quilt
Schoolhouse Wallhanging
Diamond Log Cabin Tablecloth or Treeskirt
Morning Star Quilt
Trip Around the World Quilt
Friendship Quilt
Country Christmas
Bunnies and Blossoms
Creating With Color
Dresden Plate Quilt, a Simplified Method
Pineapple Quilt, a Piece of Cake
Radiant Star Quilt

Patterns and Other Projects

Dresden Placemats and Tea Cozy
Log Cabin Wreath
Log Cabin Christmas Tree
Patchwork Santa
Flying Geese Quilt
Miniature May Basket Wallhanging
Angel of Antiquity

Videos for Rent or Purchase

Log Cabin Quilt
Bear's Paw Quilt
Monkey Wrench Quilt
Ohio Star Quilt
Lover's Knot Quilt
Amish Quilt
Irish Chain Quilt
Schoolhouse Wallhanging
Diamond Log Cabin
Morning Star Quilt
Trip Around the World
Flying Geese Quilt
Radiant Star Wallhanging
Creating With Color
Block Party Series
and more!

Supplies Available

Rotary Cutters
Rotary Replacement Blades
Cutting Mats with Grids
6" x 6" Mini Rulers
6" x 12" Rulers
6" x 24" Rulers
12 1/2" x 12 1/2" Square Up Ruler
Quilter's Pins
Magnetic Pin Holder
Magnetic Seam Guides
Curved Needles

If you are ever in Southern California, San Diego county, drop by and visit the Quilt in a Day Center. Our quilt shop and classroom is located in the La Costa Meadows Business Park. Write ahead for a current class schedule and map.

Quilt in a Day
1955 Diamond Street, San Marcos, California 92069
Order Line: 1-800- U2 KWILT(1-800-825-9458)   Information Line: 1-619-591-0081